ECHO PARK ELEMENTARY SCHOOL
ISD 196
14100 County Road 11
Burnsville, Minnesota 55337

How Do Plants Grow?

by Julie K. Lundgren

Science Content Editor:
Kristi Lew

Rourke
Educational Media

rourkeeducationalmedia.com

Science content editor: Kristi Lew
A former high school teacher with a background in biochemistry and more than 10 years of experience in cytogenetic laboratories, Kristi Lew specializes in taking complex scientific information and making it fun and interesting for scientists and non-scientists alike. She is the author of more than 20 science books for children and teachers.

www.rourkeeducationalmedia.com

Photo credits: Cover © antishock, Vaclav Volrab; Cover logo frog © Eric Pohl, test tube © Sergey Lazarev; Page 3 © Elenamiv; Page 5 © Tony Campbell; Page 7 © Filipe B. Varela; Page 9 © marema; Page 11 © Verbenko; Page 13 © David P. Smith; Page 15 © Denis Vrublevski; Page 17 © Vaclav Volrab; Page 19 © Carlos Caetano; Page 20 © Vaclav Volrab; Page 23 © J. Helgason

Editor: Kelli Hicks

Cover and page design by Nicola Stratford, bdpublishing.com

Library of Congress Cataloging-in-Publication Data

Lundgren, Julie K.
 How do plants grow? / Julie K. Lundgren.
   p. cm. -- (My science library)
 ISBN 978-1-61741-721-4 (Hard cover)
 ISBN 978-1-61741-923-2 (Soft cover)
 1. Growth (Plants)--Juvenile literature. 2. Plants--Development--Juvenile literature. I. Title.
 QK731.L95 2012
 571.8'2--dc22
                              2011003863

Rourke Educational Media
Printed in the United States of America,
North Mankato, Minnesota

rourkeeducationalmedia.com

customerservice@rourkeeducationalmedia.com • PO Box 643328 Vero Beach, Florida 32964

Almost all plants need the Sun to grow.

Most plants also need **water** and good **soil**.

Plants have many parts that help them get what they need to grow.

Most plants have **roots**.

roots

Most plants have **stems**.

stem

Roots and stems carry water from the soil to the plant.

Carrots are roots.

13

Most plants have **leaves.**

leaves

Leaves collect **sunlight**.

Green plants change sunlight, air, and water into food.

19

Plants use the food they make to live and grow.

SHOW what you know

1. Can you name the parts of a plant?

2. What do the parts do?

3. How is the Sun important to plants?

Picture Glossary

leaves (LEEVZ):
The plant part that is usually green and flat. Leaves are attached to the stem.

roots (ROOTS):
The plant part that gets water and nutrients from the soil for the whole plant to use.

soil (SOYL):
Soil is the dirt in which a plant grows. Plants get water and nutrients from the soil.

stems (STEHMZ):
Stems support the plant and carry water to the leaves from the roots.

sunlight (SUN-lite):
Plants use the Sun's energy, in the form of sunlight, to make their own food.

water (WAH-ter):
Water is the colorless liquid that falls as rain. Plants cannot live without water.

Index

Websites

www.biology4kids.com/files/plants_main.html
www.kidsgardening.org/family.asp
http://urbanext.illinois.edu/firstgarden/
www.woodmagic.vt.edu/kids/index.htm

About the Author

Julie K. Lundgren grew up near
Lake Superior where she liked to
muck about in the woods,
pick berries, and expand her rock
collection. Her interests
led her to a degree in biology.
She lives in Minnesota with
her family.

ECHO PARK ELEMENTARY SCHOOL
ISD 196
14100 County Road 11
Burnsville, Minnesota 55337